DON'T PANIC, ORGANISE!

A MUTE MAGAZINE PAMPHLET ON RECENT STRUGGLES IN EDUCATION

MUTE BOOKS 2011

MUTE PUBLISHING
46 LEXINGTON STREET
LONDON W1F OLP

MUTE@METAMUTE.ORG
METAMUTE.ORG, @MUTEMAGAZINE

Except for the images, which originally appeared elsewhere and are republished here, all content is copyright of Mute Publishing and the authors. However, Mute encourages use of its content for purposes that are non-commercial, critical, or disruptive of capitalist property relations. Please make sure you credit the author and *Mute* as the original publisher.

This legend is devised in the absence of a licence which adequately represents this book's contributors' respective position on copyright, and to acknowledge but deny the copyrighting performed by default where copyright is waived.

Design: Laura Oldenbourg
Production: Simon Worthington

ISBN: **978-1-906496-54-8**
Printed in the UK.

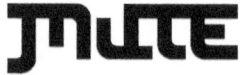

CONTENTS

INTRODUCTION   4
by *Mute* Editorial Collective

UNIVERSITY STRUGGLES AT THE END OF THE EDU-DEAL   6
by George Caffentzis

STRUGGLE AS A SECOND LANGUAGE   15
by B&R

BEYOND MEASURE   21
by Anonymous

GREAT PROTEST, SHAME ABOUT THE 'DESPICABLE MINORITY' –   26
NUS LEADERS
by Sandra Morgan

AN NUS STEWARD TRIED TO 'CLEGG' ME   28
by Heidi Liane Hasbrouck

WIDENING PARTICIPATION   34
by Anathematician

INCREASED STUDENT FEES CONSTITUTE A SOCIALLY PROGRESSIVE   39
GRADUATE TAX IN ALL BUT NAME"
"TAKEN FROM 'FREQUENTLY ASSERTED FALLACIES OF THE CRISIS
AND HOW TO QUASH THEM'
by the *Mute* Collective and Danny Hayward

DON'T PANIC, ORGANISE!
A MUTE MAGAZINE PAMPHLET ON RECENT STRUGGLES IN EDUCATION

The cuts, lay-offs and tuition-fee hikes that are besetting higher and further education internationally are undoubtedly a direct response to financial crisis and its ricocheting bomb of personal, commercial and national debt. But they also have deeper roots. They should be understood as part of the more gradual process of what George Caffentzis, in his analysis of the international situation, calls the 'breakdown of the edu-deal'; the inability for capital, and therefore the state, to pay for the costs of producing a well educated workforce or to guarantee that investment in education will result in a more vigorous economy and increased living standards for those with qualifications.

This breakdown, and the dogmatism of free market economics which seeks to alleviate it, has seen the imposition of a business rationale onto what previously had been regarded as the provision of a public service, sometimes even a public good in the UK and across Europe. From the investment of endowment funds on the market, to the conversion of students into (badly ripped off) consumers, to the no-frills fixed-term contracts being doled out to staff, to the speculative purchase of the future IP generated by scientific and technical departments, to the intended exchangeability of all qualifications under the Bologna Process, education is being ever more deeply determined by free market principles.

With the ground changing this fast under staff and students' feet, the ability for collective action to fight the savage rounds of cuts has itself suffered as a result of a generalised precarity and fragmentation. *Mute*'s interview with two organisers of last summer's strike at Tower Hamlets College reminds us that attacks on education workers and students are not soley motivated by financial concerns, but also comprise an attack on our working culture (our rights, values and expectations more generally). Despite the hostile conditions, we have nevertheless seen a persistent and recently growing wave of strikes, actions and occupations, both wildcat and union co-ordinated, breaking out around the world. Sixth formers, students, staff and those with a less personal stake in education are uniting in a new plane of struggle. However, a number of the reports included here stress the growing tension between the particularity of the cuts to the education sector and the more general 'public sector fight back' that is emerging. Despite the need to recognise the distinctions within the education sector itself (between academic staff and students on one hand, and non-academic staff on the other) there is a distinct danger of forming a coalition solely amongst students and workers who used to be students.

The student occupation at Middlesex University over the summer of 2010, as well as the more recent spate of occupations and sit-ins in universities, schools, art galleries and other public spaces across Britain, have nevertheless ushered in a moment full of potential. Not only have they sought to be inclusive, but they have also shown the growing irrelevance of student leaders and old style mass-organising. Heidi Liane Hasbrouck's piece on the NUS's denunciation of the Millbank riot highlights this moment of self-realisation. There is a widening recognition of a need to self-organise and continually push at the borders of the possible. This is not '68 redux; and a better thing for it.

All of this begs the question, will this fight-back be enough to save any residual quality and equality within education and its institutions? *Mute* began compiling a mini-dossier of reports, questionnaires and analyses on the crisis and struggles within education in May 2010, as it was unfolding in the UK and beyond. Since the magnificent occupation of the Tory headquarters at Millbank on 9 November – which seemed to jolt people out of their despair or slumbers – many more reports on education struggles have been published in *Mute*. Here we present you with a selection of some of the most urgent.

UNIVERSITY STRUGGLES AT THE END OF THE EDU-DEAL
BY GEORGE CAFFENTZIS

As students around the world start to take action against national governments' university spending cuts, George Caffentzis sees a plane of struggle developing; one which acts against the crooked deal of high cost education exchanged for life-long precarity

> We should not ask for the university to be destroyed, nor for it to be preserved. We should not ask for anything. We should ask ourselves and each other to take control of these universities, collectively, so that education can begin.
>
> - From a flyer found in the Vienna Academy of Fine Arts originally written in the University of California

Since the massive student revolt in France, in 2006, against the Contrat Première Embauche (CPE), and the 'anomalous wave' in Italy in 2008, student protest has mounted in almost every part of the world, suggesting a reprise of the heady days of 1968. It reached a crescendo in the Fall and Winter of 2009 when campus strikes and occupations proliferated from California to Austria, Germany, Croatia, Switzerland and later the UK. The website Tinyurl.com/squatted-universities counted 168 universities (mostly in Europe) where actions took place between 20 October and the end of December 2009. And the surge is far from over. On 4 March 2010, in the US, on the occasion of a nationwide day of action (the first since May 1970) called in defense of public education, one of the co-ordinating organisations listed 64 different campuses that saw some form of protest.[1] On the same day, the South African Students' Congress (SASCO) tried to close down nine universities calling for free university education. The protest at the University of Johannesburg proved

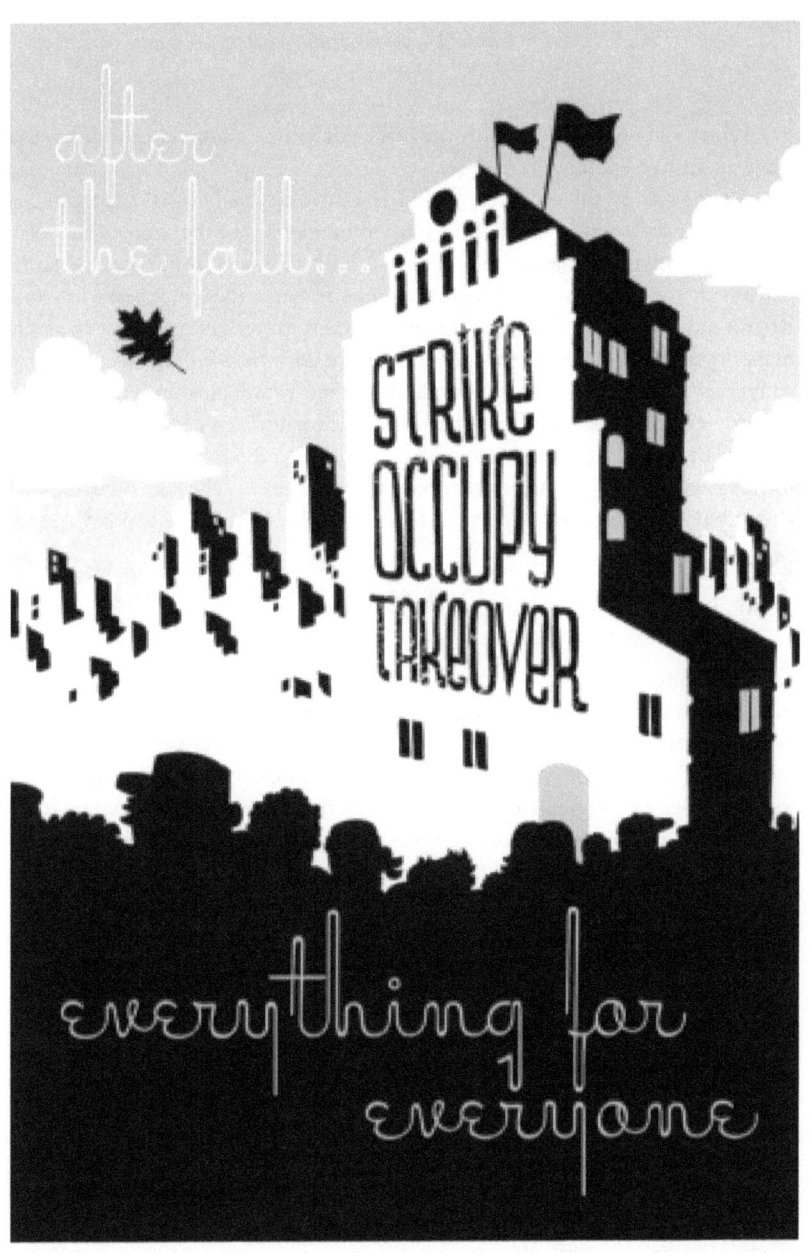

IMAGE: Cover of *After the Fall: Communiques from Occupied California*, February 2010

to be the most contentious, with the police driving students away with water cannons from a burning barricade.

At the root of the most recent mobilisations are the budget cuts that governments and academic institutions have implemented in the wake of the Wall Street meltdown and the tuition hikes that have followed from them; up to 32 percent in the University of California system, and similar increases in some British universities. In this light, the new student movement can be seen as the main organised response to the global financial crisis. Indeed, 'We won't pay for your crisis' - the slogan of striking Italian students - has become an international battle cry. But the economic crisis has exacerbated a general dissatisfaction that has deeper sources, stemming from the neoliberal reform of education and the restructuring of production that have taken place over the last three decades, which have affected every aspect of student life throughout the world.[2]

THE END OF THE EDU-DEAL

The most outstanding elements of this restructuring have been the corporatisation of the university systems and the commercialisation of education. 'For profit' universities are still a minority on the academic scene but the 'becoming business' of academe is well advanced especially in the US, where it dates back to the passing of the Bayh-Dole Act of 1980, that enabled universities to apply for patents for 'discoveries' made in their labs that companies would have to pay to use. Since then, the restructuring of academe as a money-making venture has proceeded unabated. The opening of university labs to private enterprise, the selling of knowledge on the world market (through online education and off-shore teaching), the precarisation of academic labour and introduction of constantly rising tuition fees forcing students to plunge ever further into debt, have become standard features of the US academic life, and with regional differences the same trends can now be registered worldwide.

In Europe, the struggle epitomising the new student movement has been against the 'Bologna Process', an EU project that institutes a European Higher Education Area, and promotes the circulation of labour within its territory through the homogenisation and standardisation of schooling programs and degrees. The Bologna Process unabashedly places the university at the service of business. It redefines education as the production of mobile and flexible workers, possessing the skills employers require; it centralises the creation of pedagogical standards, removes control from local actors, and devalues local knowledge and local concerns. Similar developments have been taking place in many university systems in Africa and Asia (like Taiwan, Singapore, Japan) that also are being 'Americanised' and standardised (for example, in Taiwan through the imposition of the Social Science Citation Index to evaluate professors) - so that global corporations can use Indian, Russian, South African or Brazilian, instead of US or EU 'knowledge workers', with the confidence that they are fit for the job.[3]

It is generally recognised that the commercialisation of the university system has partly been a response to the student struggles and social movements of the '60s and '70s, which marked the end of the education policy that had prevailed in the Keynesian era. As campus after campus, from Berkeley to Berlin, became the hotbed of an anti-authoritarian revolt, dispelling the Keynesian illusion that investment in college education would pay down the line in the form of an increase in the general productivity of work, the ideology of education as preparation to civic life and a public good had to be discarded.[4]

But the new neoliberal regime also represented the end of a class deal. With the elimination of stipends, allowances, and free tuition, the cost of 'education', i.e. the cost of preparing oneself for work, has been imposed squarely on the work-force, in what amounts to a massive wage-cut, that is particularly onerous considering that precarity has become the dominant work relation, and that, like any other commodity, the knowledge 'bought' is quickly devalued by technological innovation. It is also the end of the role of the state as mediator. Students in the corporatised university now confront capital directly, in the crowded classrooms where teachers can hardly match names on the rosters with faces, in the expansion of adjunct teaching and, above all, in the mounting student debt which, by turning students into indentured servants to the banks and/or state, acts as a disciplinary mechanism on student life, also casting a long shadow on their future.

Still, through the 1990s, student enrolment continued to grow across the world under the pressure of an economic restructuring making education a condition for employment. It became a mantra, during the last two decades, from New York to Paris to Nairobi, to claim that with the rise of the 'knowledge

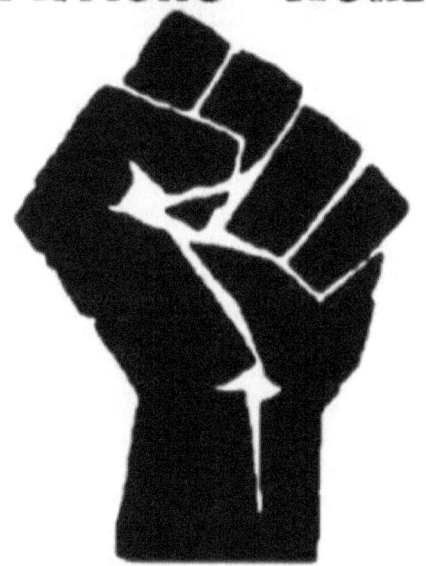

society' and information revolution, cost what it may, college education is a 'must' (World Bank 2002). Statistics seemed to confirm the wisdom of climbing the education ladder, pointing to an 83 percent differential in the US between the wages of college graduates and those of workers with high school degrees. But the increase in enrolment and indebtedness must also be read as a form of struggle, a rejection of the restrictions imposed by the subjection of

IMAGE: Anarchist student solidarity poster

education to the logic of the market, a hidden form of appropriation, manifesting itself in time through the increase in the numbers of those defaulting on their loan repayments.

There is no doubt, in this context, that the global financial crisis of 2008 targets this strategy of resistance, removing, through budget cutbacks, lay-offs, and the massification of unemployment, the last remaining guarantees. Certainly the 'edu-deal', that promised higher wages and work satisfaction in exchange for workers and their families taking on the cost for higher education, is dissolving as well. In the crisis capital is reneging on this 'deal', certainly because of the proliferation of defaults and because capitalism today refuses any guarantees, such as the promise of high wages to future knowledge workers.

The university financial crisis (the tuition fee increases, budget cutbacks, furloughs and lay-offs) is directly aimed at eliminating the wage guarantee that formal higher education was supposed to bring and at taming the 'cognitariat'. As in the case of immigrant workers, the attack on the students does not signify that knowledge workers are not needed, but rather that they need to be further disciplined and proletarianised, through an attack on the power they have begun to claim partly because of their position in the process of accumulation.

Student rebellion is therefore deep-seated, with the prospect of debt slavery being compounded by a future of insecurity and a sense of alienation from an institution perceived to be mercenary and bureaucratic that, into the bargain, produces a commodity subject to rapid devaluation.

DEMANDS OR OCCUPATIONS?

The student movement, however, faces a political problem, most evident in the US and, to a lesser extent, in Europe. The movement has two souls. On the one side, it demands free university education, reviving the dream of publicly financed 'mass scholarity', ostensibly proposing to return to the model of the Keynesian era. On the other, it is in revolt against the university itself, calling for a mass exit from it or aiming to transform the campus into a base for alternative knowledge production that is accessible to those outside its 'walls'.[5]

This dichotomy, which some characterise as a return to the 'reform versus revolution' disputes of the past, has become most visible in the debate sparked off during the University of California strikes last year, over 'demands' versus 'occupations', which at times has taken an acrimonious tone, as these terms have become complex signifiers for hierarchies and identities, differential power relations, and consequences for risk taking.

The contrast is not purely ideological. It is rooted in the contradictions facing every antagonistic movement today. Economic restructuring has fragmented the workforce, deepened divisions and, not least, it has increased the effort and time required for daily reproduction. A student population holding two or three jobs is less prone to organise than its more affluent peers in the '60s.

At the same time there is a sense, among many, that there is nothing more to negotiate, that demands have become superfluous since, for the majority of students, acquiring a certificate is no guarantee for the future which promises simply more precarity and constant self-recycling. Many students realise that capitalism has nothing to offer this generation, that no 'new deal' is possible, even in the metropolitan areas of the world, where most wealth is accumulated. Though there is a widespread temptation to revive it, the Keynesian interest group politics of making demands and 'dealing' is long dead.

Thus the slogan 'occupy everything': occupying buildings being seen as a means of self-empowerment, the creation of spaces that students can control, a break in the flow of work and value through which the university expands its reach, and the production of a 'counter-power' prefigurative of the communalising relations students today want to construct.

It is hard to know how the 'demands/occupation' conflict within the student movement will be resolved. What is certain is that this is a major challenge the movement must overcome in order to increase its power and its capacity to connect with other struggles. This will be a necessary step if the movement is to gain the power to reclaim education from the hands of the academic authorities and the state. As a next step there is presently much discussion about creating 'knowledge commons', in the sense of creating forms of autonomous knowledge production, not finalised or conditioned by the market and open to those outside the campus walls.

Meanwhile, as *Edu-Notes* has recognised,

> already the student movement is creating a common of its own in the very process of the struggle. At the speed of light, news of the strikes, rallies, and occupations, have circulated around the world prompting a global electronic tam-tam of exchanged communiqués, slogans, messages of solidarity and support, resulting in an exceptional volume of images, documents, stories.[6]

Yet, the main 'common' the movement will have to construct is the extension of its mobilisation to other workers in the crisis. Key to this construction will be the issue of the debt that is the arch 'anti-common', since it is the transformation of collective surplus that could be used for the liberation of workers into a tool of their enslavement. Abolition of the student debt can be the connective tissue between the movement and the others struggling against foreclosures in the US and the larger movement against sovereign debt internationally.

ACKNOWLEDGEMENTS

I want to thank the students and faculty I recently interviewed from the University of California, the Academy of Fine Arts in Vienna and Rhodes University in South Africa for sharing their knowledge. I also want to thank my comrades in the Edu-Notes group for their insights and inspiration.

George Caffentzis <gcaffentz@aol.com> is a member of the *Midnight Notes Collective*. Together with the collective, he has co-edited two books, *Midnight Oil: Work Energy War 1973-1992* and *Auroras of the Zapatistas: Local and Global Struggles in the Fourth World War*. Both were published by Autonomedia Press

FOOTNOTES

1. See, http://defendeducation.org

2. Edu-Factory Collective, *Towards a Global Autonomous University*, Brooklyn, NY: Autonomedia, 2009.

3. See, Silvia Federici, George Caffentzis, Ousseina Alidou, *A Thousand Flowers: Social Struggles Against Structural Adjustment in African Universities*, Trenton, NJ: Africa World Press, 2000, Richard Pithouse, *Asinamali: University Struggles in Post-Apartheid South Africa*, Trenton: Africa World Press, 2006 and Arthur Hou-ming Huang, 'Science as Ideology: SSCI, TSSCI and the Evaluation System of Social Sciences in Taiwan', *Inter-Asia Cultural Studies*, Volume 10 2009, Number 2, pp. 282-291.

4. George Caffentzis, 'Throwing Away the Ladder: The Universities in the Crisis', *Zerowork* I, 1975, pp. 128-142.

5. *After the Fall: Communiqués from Occupied California*, 2010, Accessed at www.afterthefallcommuniques.info

6. *Edu-Notes*, 'Introduction to *Edu-Notes*', unpublished manuscript.

STRUGGLE AS A SECOND LANGUAGE
BY B&R

While last summer's strike at Tower Hamlets College is often portrayed as a victory by unions, two of its organisers, B&R, remain critical, and place ESOL at the butt end of the government's chauvinist austerity

MUTE: Can you summarise the events surrounding the strike last year? What caused it and how was it resolved?

B&R: Briefly, a new principal came to Tower Hamlets College and 4 months later, on 5 June, issued us with a document giving us notice that we were facing massive cuts in provision and the loss of 40-60 teaching and support jobs in 30 days (the minimum days required under law for this many job losses). There had been some warning that something was up, so our union branch (UCU) had already opened an official dispute that meant we could apply for a strike ballot right away. Our local union branch had a long tradition of very practical, decentralised organising and this meant people were involved in large numbers right away. A massive campaign swung into action resulting in a unanimous vote for indefinite strike action from the first working day after the summer, when students were enrolling for the new academic year. We were on strike for 4 weeks, with very solid picket lines, brilliant support locally and beyond, daily strike committee meetings open to everyone, and weekly mass assemblies where we made the big decisions.

We had been in official dispute over compulsory redundancies, and the officially negotiated settlement was that 7 people had 'volunteered' to accept their compulsory redundancy notices. These people were under tremendous pressure - 4 weeks of negotiations had got us nowhere. We feel now that we did not do enough to convince these people that the strike was not about the other strikers making sacrifices to help them - it was about them going through hell in order to support everyone else.

MUTE: It's been a few months since the end of the strike and that partial victory which concluded it. Has the situation stabilised?

B&R: Now that we're back, what we suspected has been confirmed: that the attack was not motivated by financial consideration, rather Management wanted to attack the strength of the union and our working culture. Part of that is to do with pay and conditions but it's also to do with the type of education teaching and learning that Tower Hamlets is known for.[1]

Workload has increased, union room to manoeuvre is under attack, crèche provision under threat, pressure from managers to kick people off courses if they are pregnant, ill, or otherwise 'at risk of not succeeding' (i.e. achieving an external qualification), and we are waiting to see what the government's massive cuts in adult education will mean. Already the Union has been asked by Senior Management to promote voluntary redundancies as a means to reduce compulsories but this won't happen.

Adult education is generally facing potentially catastrophic cuts this and next year.

MUTE: Has the atmosphere among teachers and students changed since the strike ended?

B&R: We teach adult English for Speakers of Other Languages, so we don't know much about the 6th form or other adult provisions, but our students are still interested in talking about the cuts and the strike, and know how important it was. By and large students were very supportive of the strike and there was a lot of involvement, but little autonomous organising by students. Now students know they are lucky to have classes, and will fight with us again when the time comes. Watch out for actions around the loss of crèches (and therefore the possibility of studying for many women) coming up.

Among teachers, people are demoralised by working under a Senior Management that has nothing but contempt for us. We also know that much of it is coming from the government and that we have already lost a lot of ground, for

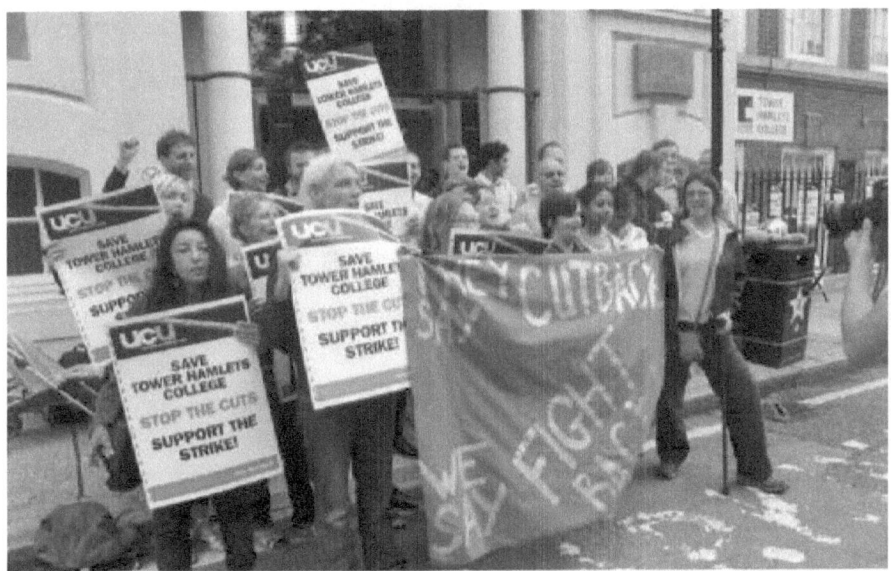

example, ESOL teachers are now highly implicated in systems of immigration control due to the language requirements for citizenship and settlement. But, because of the incredible solidarity generated during the strike, both outside and inside the college, we also feel strong. There's nothing like standing on a picket line with people for four weeks to make you feel connected to the people you work with. We all know each other now, and I think have good relations with the support staff who did not strike but helped us out when they could.

MUTE: Are the cuts part of a larger pattern of restructuring further education? Do they connect to an intensification of administrative work and management and a loss of educational values?

B&R: Certainly. During the strike we were so focussed on the job losses and therefore maybe did not focus on the broader issues around education. Talk of 'making links' and of the 'public sector fight back' can sometimes obscure what is distinctive about the education sector.

IMAGE: Strikers in front of the College

Our funding is now linked to targets, and the struggle right now is not to internalise the model of target driven education. Management needs us to accept the logic of doing everything we can to secure ongoing funding by teaching to the test and getting the results, even though almost all teachers will say that this means teaching and learning is largely replaced by exam training.

It is probably easier to fight on the terrain of job losses than over the multitude of large and small issues to do with the content of our jobs. The fact that we got through the strike as strong as we did means we are now better placed to fight for these things, but we also know we have to try to keep educational values central to what we do - the Unions have largely given up this fight, but teachers haven't.

MUTE: The proverbial axe fell hard on Tower Hamlets' ESOL courses, but ESOL seems threatened at Manchester College, Hackney Community College, Solihall College in West Midlands and generally nation-wide. What do you make of this impression that ESOL is, if not expendable, reducible? Why do level 1 courses seem most at risk?

B&R: ESOL is incredibly political, situated as it is at the intersection of various government agendas. ESOL teachers are expected to not only teach language, but to deliver social cohesion, employability and citizenship. The burden of what it's thought ESOL must do keeps growing, but with less funding and in an increasingly restrictive audit culture.

The general plan is to move Entry Level ESOL away from FE colleges and have them provided by Councils, training agencies, charities, and voluntary organisations. Some of these other providers are excellent, but many are shoddy. Pay and conditions are usually worse, but more teachers will be isolated, working without support of other teachers. Students lose out not only on the expertise of highly skilled teachers working in a collaborative atmosphere, but also on the resources, support services and clear routes of progression they can get in a college.

At a recent talk about the history and politics of ESOL, Alice Robson pointed out that the government tries to avoid looking like it's spending money on immigrants. It would like much of it to be taken over by the private agencies and the Third Sector. While the professional qualifications ESOL teachers need are now quite high, it actually looks like we're heading back to the days when ESOL was taught by volunteers.

The plan to make employers contribute to the costs of ESOL (Train to Gain) has been a complete failure. The recession and the fact that there are no jobs seem not to have caused a rethink on pushing 'employability' at ever-lower levels.

The Government's New Approach to ESOL claims to aim funding at the most vulnerable and also under-represented (ethnic) groups but there is no increase in money so this means withdrawing provision from some. For example, in Tower Hamlets there is apparently not enough take up by young Somali men, so the plan is to target them - and reduce the number of Bengali women receiving ESOL.

This all sounds grim but, completely against the tide, there are a few exciting things around, for example the Freire-ian 'Reflect for Esol' project which now has some funding to train teachers in this tradition of radical pedagogy.

MUTE: Given that during the strike, there seemed to be dissension between the Arbour/Bethnal Green campus and the Poplar campus, is that still an issue?

B&R: The splits don't seem so significant right now, I'm glad to say. At any rate, whatever happens next has to be on a national level. I would expect the same issues that caused dissension to arise as they always do: how to work and make decisions collectively, how to organise anti-hierarchically, how to relate to workers in other unions/non-unionised workers, when to operate by the book and when to oppose Union legality, and so on. I guess these issues arise during any workplace struggle and can't be addressed except in practice.

MUTE: Were there limits with organising in and around UCU and what were they? Is there hope for a meaningful nation-wide organisation to preserve ESOL, given the problems you faced? How necessary would national organisation be?

B&R: Yes, there were limits - it was difficult at first as we were catapulted into a situation that few of us really understood. Now it is clear that once we decided to enter into negotiations with management and UCU we were accepting a compromise deal/outcome - by the very nature of negotiating in that way. The alternative would be to refuse to negotiate - that may have given us more power. However, were we ready to take that step? Would we have had any more than a minority of the branch behind this and if not how limiting would that have been?

For UCU, the most important things were maintaining the branches - being able to walk back to work with heads held high, as we were often told. UCU national wanted us as a showcase, taking on a maverick new Senior Management and winning. For this they were willing to pay us a wage of £50 per day. Strike pay is a pretty awesome thing and without it we couldn't have kept going for 4 weeks, but it may also have limited certain possibilities. All the creative chaos of self-organisation that made the strike so exciting - the open meetings, vibrant picket lines, direct actions and social events seemed in real contrast to the negotiations during which nothing was achieved for almost 4 weeks.

UCU were not the slightest bit interested in what the strikers really wanted - the jobs back, and with it, the same sense that it was not for nothing that our colleagues had been dragged through months of hell and humiliation before losing their jobs.

UCU officials had already decided before the final strike meeting that the strike was over - their role was in great contrast to the initial rallying call of the first assembly. They made bald statements of fact such as 'your trade dispute is over' before the vote on the deal. The strike which had been fought in the spirit of participation and debate was shut down in a predictably authoritarian way.

In the event only a minority voted to stay on strike but a lot of people couldn't equate the sense of strength that we had had with the deal that had been struck. In fact few understood the deal. There was no real sense that we'd won or what we'd done in our branch, despite what has been portrayed.

What we do have is the collective memory of the strike and how we did things. Definitely whatever happens next in adult education should involve national organisation, and we can only hope it's going to be possible to push pass the limits of UCU.

Becky and Rebecca are adult ESOL teachers at Tower Hamlets College.

FOOTNOTE

1. An account of a mass refusal of management discipline around teaching culture can be found here: http://thecommune.wordpress.com/2009/10/13/workers-revolt-against-vygotsky-an-account-of-unofficial-action-at-tower-hamlets-college/

BEYOND MEASURE
BY ANONYMOUS

In the aftermath of an unsuccessful student occupation and the impending closure of Middlesex University's Philosophy Department, a student-occupier advocates the tactics of immeasurability as a way of counteracting the terminal managerialism of branded universities

> *The best foundation for a competitive economy starts with an education and training system that gives workers the skills they need for the jobs of the 21st century - this philosophy is at the core of Middlesex Organisational Development Network.*
>
> - Middlesex University Website, 2010

With such a rationale it is hardly surprising that Middlesex management decided to close their philosophy department.[1] Like any other business, the production of workers for the jobs of the 21st century means eliminating anything that does not contribute. The philosophy department, which, in their words, made 'no measurable contribution', had to go.

The Save Middlesex Philosophy campaign responded, 'we are measurable! And we measure up well! Look at the RAE ratings, look at the postgraduate numbers, look at all the big names who like us, look at all the little names on the petition, look at the number of hits on the site, look at the amount of articles in the *Guardian*...' But when you start speaking in numbers, you have already lost. Perhaps academics - in order to remain academics - have to do this. But those of us who will not find jobs on the other side of our studies have less to lose. We can refuse their limits and the people that guard them. We can counter them by refusing to be counted. We can be unmeasurable.

When, in protest against the closure, students occupied the main building on campus, we experienced moments of this refusal: defying security guards on the doors; telling the student union president to leave and resisting her attempts to 'represent' us; refusing to give names; rejecting management's requests to be reasonable; expanding the occupation from one room to the whole building; forcing security to get out; climbing onto the roof; eating together in a lecture hall; hanging banners out of the windows; rejecting leaders, formal procedures and party politics. Every limit we broke made it easier to break the next one. And finally management capitulated and came to our door to beg us for a meeting. We rejected their offer and they ran to the High Court.

But let's not romanticise things: many limits remained firmly in place, or reappeared as we lost confidence. We allowed ourselves to be negotiated with, talked about excellence, big names, numbers, the media... At times, we even drifted into discussions over whether limits were there for a reason. After all, wasn't our health and safety dependent on counting people in and out, on having barricades that didn't block fire exits, on staying off the roof? And didn't our personal property depend on cordoned-off areas, guarded with bodies and locks? Isolated as we were from other struggles - at the end of term, on the edges of London, before cuts became national - it was difficult for people not to start doubting themselves. These doubts became fatal when we received the High Court injunction, frightening most people into leaving. Reduced to only 15, we felt we could no longer hold the building and left the next day. As the management regained control, the occupation went from being indefinite to being only 12 days long. It went from being our building to being their building. Our banners were taken from the roof, our barricades were thrown out and people went back to work.

Yet things weren't the same for us. The following weeks included a defiance of the injunction in a night-long occupation of the library, a camp outside the university headquarters in protest at staff and student suspensions, and a disruption of a Middlesex art show; all of which helped rebuild some sense of the power we had had during the occupation.

Then the tutors announced that postgraduates would have to move to Kingston University to finish their studies, while undergraduates would stay on at Middlesex. Management got exactly what they wanted: a splitting of the department, a moving of most of the troublemakers to another institution, and the reminder that, when it comes to numbers, it is the tutors and not

A MUTE MAGAZINE PAMPHLET ON RECENT STRUGGLES IN EDUCATION

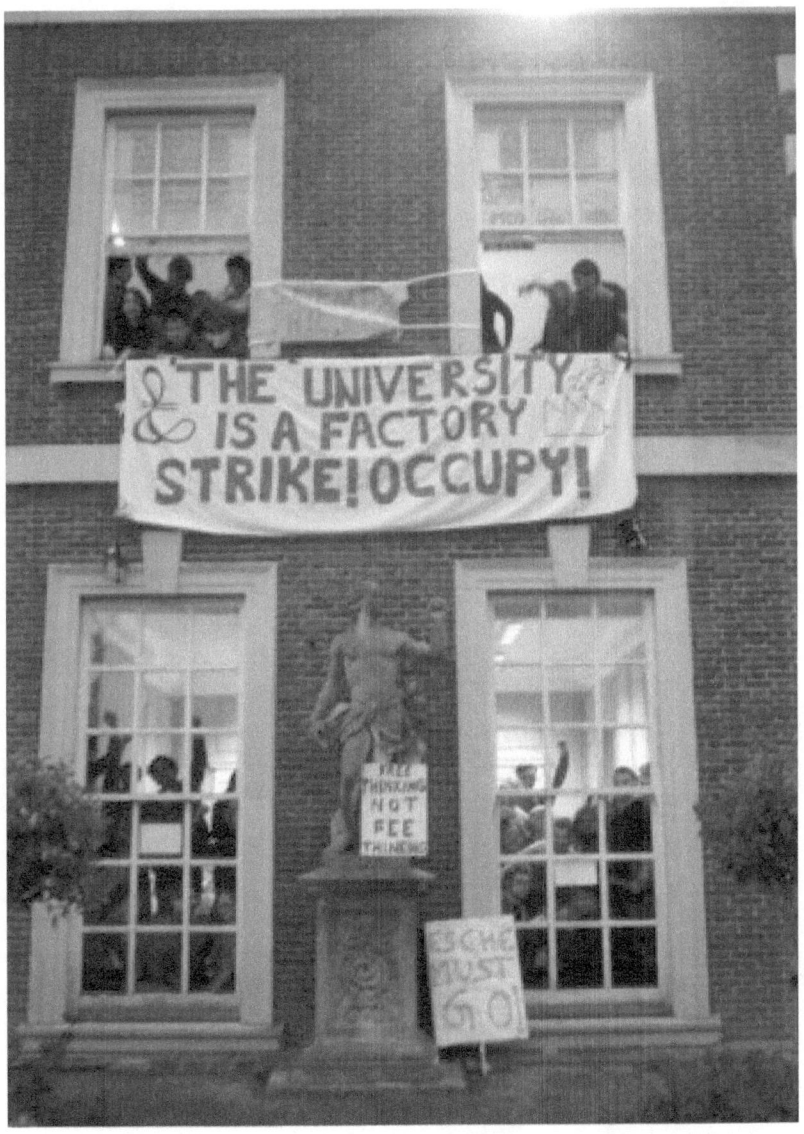

IMAGE: students occupy the executive boardroom on Middlesex University's Trent Park campus

students who make the decisions. The tutors even claimed that this move to the other side of London, losing a third of their colleagues and all of their undergraduates, was all a 'partial victory', and that Kingston University proved that 'another way is possible'. However, although Kingston might have been convinced by the department's measurability, might have seen this 'world-renowned' centre as a good investment - without undergraduates - we are kidding ourselves if we don't think it is under the same pressure as Middlesex to drop departments once the prestige and money stop rolling in. True, Kingston might be slightly less brutal, and less brutally honest than Middlesex, but Middlesex managers are not just rogue bullies. They are holding the torch for an approach to education that stretches across the country - even, dare we say it, to Kingston.

There are times and places in which philosophy is profitable: in the Russell Group universities (an affiliation of 20 leading UK universities) it bolsters an elite who feel further justified in their power because they've read books apparently incomprehensible to everyone else; and at polytechnics, once upon a time, it did a good job of channelling potentially dangerous questions into benign grades. However, as the competitive economy becomes the answer to everything, such questions stop being a threat. The battleground shifts from one of ideas to one of practice: when the economy is in crisis, when work is increasingly hard to come by and resistance a rising possibility, those universities that are not reproducing the elite must produce workers that are as submissive, as measurable, and as controllable as possible.

Slightly repetitively, Middlesex prides itself on, 'learning that provides a flexible learning experience that is delivered through work, in work, for work.' It has not only set up Middlesex Organisational Development Network - 'the first UK university-led network focusing on engagement with employers' - but it has put millions into an 'Institute for Work Based Learning'. This is used by businesses who want to 'grow their staff quickly,' and workers who want to 'catch their vision.' (What you do with a vision once it has been caught is unclear - presumably you kill it, cook it and eat it. What you do with your staff once they have been 'grown' is also unclear - presumably you kill them, cook them and eat them too.) Middlesex also recognises that 'more and more of our students will have a career that spans the world.' A true multinational, it was one of the first British universities to open campuses overseas

- in Dubai's 'Knowledge Village', in Mauritius and now in Delhi. You've got to give it to them, Middlesex management are putting the 'philosophy' of the competitive economy into practice.

So we must recognise this new terrain and fight them at Middlesex, Kingston and elsewhere - not through graphs and numbers and negotiations, but through practical activity. We must stop trying to speak their language, to be measured in our response, to settle for their compromises and their limits. Even if the occupation at Middlesex gave us only a few moments of something else, it allowed us to see that we can go further and further still, as more and more people are drawn into these struggles. We must attack them in ways that hurt them most, by pushing beyond, by doing things that are unmeasurable, unlimited, uncontrollable, uncountable and unaccountable. And we must always ensure, as the Middlesex philosophy department has failed to do, that we make 'no measurable contribution'.

FOOTNOTE

1. Although the university announced that the department will close and that there will be no further recruitment, they also decided that they would 'teach the courses out' for students still enrolled in the department.

GREAT PROTEST, SHAME ABOUT THE 'DESPICABLE MINORITY' – NUS LEADERS
BY SANDRA MORGAN

The student storming of the Tory headquarters in London was a spontaneous, mass action, proving the complete irrelevance of 'student leaders'

From the start of Wednesday's march, it was clear that this wasn't your average NUS demo. People refused to be corralled in barriers, breaking them open to take both sides of the street. Large groups of students marched away from the prescribed route, and there were clashes with police at the Department for Business Innovation and Skills.

But it was at the Tory headquarters that the anger really found itself. Thousands of people entered the courtyard, fires were lit, flares were let off, and everyone pushed towards the building. It was only the force of these thousands pushing forward that made it possible to break police lines and get in through the door.

After about forty people had managed to get in, those outside started to break the windows. Every smash was met by a loud cheer from the crowd, making it clear that these were not isolated actions but an expression of the rage of the thousands who were there.

When the windows finally broke open, the crowd surged forward, filling the foyer with people. From there, some took to the stairs, rushing to the roof, led by no-one and moving together.

Those involved were not reducible to some 'type', but were thousands of students from Further Education colleges and universities across the country, fighting together for the first time. This show of spontaneous strength from a mass of different people can only be repeated again and again in other struggles across the country in the months to come.

Meanwhile, NUS President Aaron Porter was denouncing what happened as 'despicable', saying that a perfectly nice demonstration had been 'hijacked' by a 'small minority'.

If students didn't know what side the NUS was on before, then they did now. We must thank Mr Porter for doing a very good job of making it clear just how irrelevant his union is.

And even those 'student leaders' who got on the telly purporting to represent those in the building have proved themselves to be completely disconnected from what happened. Rather than defending the forced entry into the building, one student union president argued that people went in because 'the doors were open.' Instead of saying why what happened was important in itself, they preferred to discuss the completely irrelevant issue of whether or not Nick Clegg keeps his promises.

While the mass of students are breaking through barriers, the 'student leaders' are stuck in some television studio with Jeremy Paxman. We should be more than happy to leave them there.

These 'leaders' will no doubt dream of the recent golden age of student demos, when people repeated tired slogans back to NUS megaphones, and union executives got a comfortable ride to the Labour party. But those days are gone. We now know our strength. And the NUS is not part of it.

AN NUS STEWARD TRIED TO 'CLEGG' ME
BY HEIDI LIANE HASBROUCK

'Clegging' - a masterful way of making repressive measures look fair and cuddly - is a tactic spreading to the NUS. Heidi Liane Hasbrouck isn't fooled, and argues the students' union should be radicalised or scrapped

What became clear from the student protest on cuts on 10th November is that the NUS has assimilated the Liberal Democrat political strategy. This can be seen in two peculiar events I experienced on the protest. The first event literally happened at a crossroads. After crawling along with the march for a couple of hours my friends and I decided to push along the sides to see what was really going on in Parliament Square and beyond. Pre-march rumours that there would be a sit in at the Tory HQ had us swoop by the sit-in at Parliament Square. We found ourselves standing at the roundabout at Lambeth Bridge. With protesters coming and going in different directions, we didn't know where to go so we hovered like lost tourists.

It was in this confused moment that we were approached by a friendly steward. She kindly informed us that the protest was over and there was no point of going any further. She explained the protest was larger than anticipated by the NUS and police, that the speeches had happened already and now the police were turning everyone around. I asked, 'Well where is the protest *supposed* to go to? Isn't it supposed to continue past this point?' She responded 'There's a party at LSE tonight! A post protest party!' To which I retorted, 'I wasn't asking where the party was, I am asking where the protest is!' She looked at me bemused and not prepared for the confrontation. At this moment two police riot vans screeched around the corner and hurtled down Millbank. I glanced down at her nametag - she was from the NUS (National Union of Students). So we went down to Millbank.

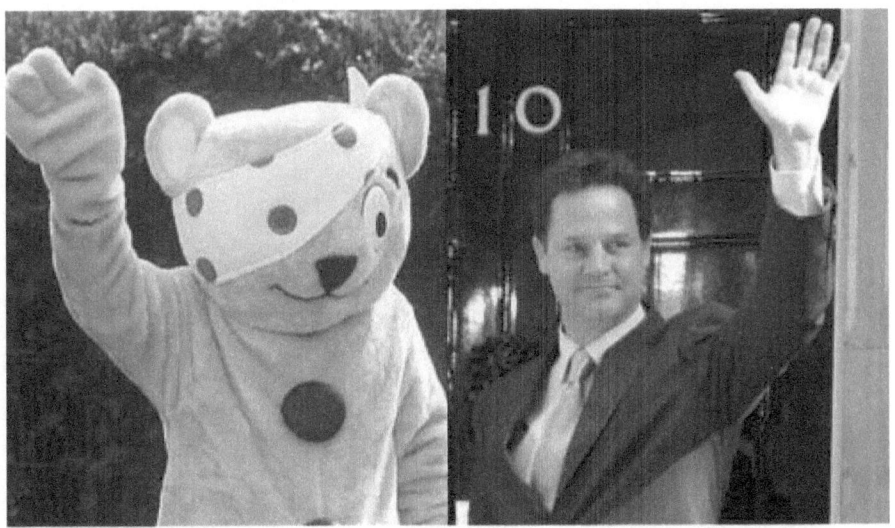

What proceeded will be written about in both the mainstream and alternative press for weeks to come. A very large group of protestors smashing in the glass windows of Millbank Tower and successfully occupying it for hours while thousands of us chanted in support. By 8pm the last 200 students would be rounded up and released one by one having to give their names, addresses, birthdays and video taken of the front and backs of their fresh faces. I will leave the analysis of this to others.

The second peculiar event was when a group of students supporting this occupation at Millbank Tower were woo'ed by an NUS representative on a megaphone rationally explaining, 'Everyone has done a great job but the protest is over now. There is nothing happening here anymore. There is an after-party at LSE starting. Come to the party at LSE!' The 'nothing to see here folks' approach of the megaphone preacher dissipated about one third of the exhausted, cold crowd. What I want to write about is the friendly steward and the megaphone party preacher.

It was at these two moments that I felt the most deflated. I expect police officers to push me in a different direction. I expect the mainstream media to

DON'T PANIC, ORGANISE

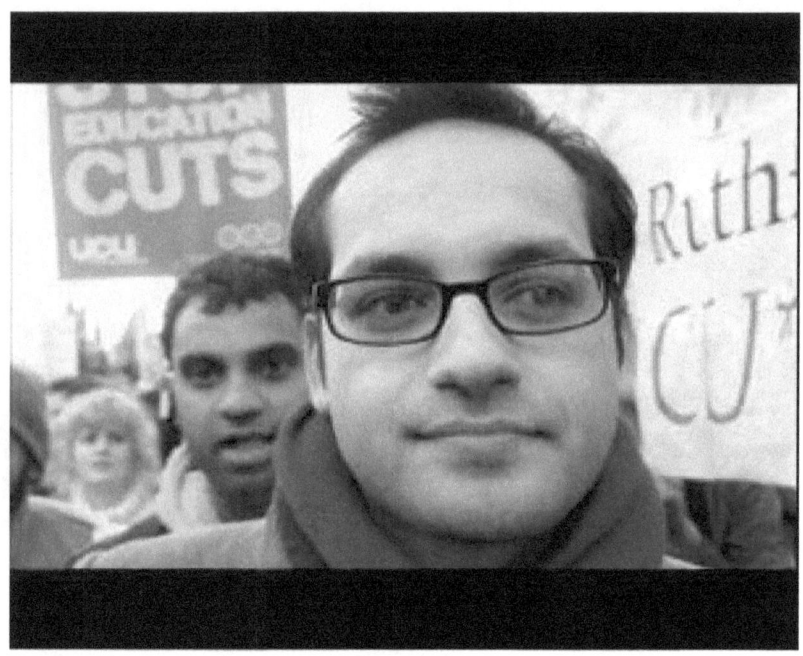

ignore the cause and focus on the injured *female* police officer. But purposeful lying by the NUS to sabotage the direct action protest spontaneously taking place at Millbank? As Charlie Brooker quipped, the NUS steward and megaphone party preacher tried to '*clegg* me'. But I refused to be clegged into believing everything was fine and a party at LSE was better than direct action. The same can be said for the thousands of other students that participated in the occupation of Millbank Tower. We wont be clegged! So what does this mean for students?

We are not only fighting a battle with the government, we are fighting against the very people that are supposed to represent us. While a lot of pre-protest rhetoric dismissed the NUS as a dying union for career minded future politicians, there was still respect for their organising abilities. It was, after all, the NUS that organised the protest. My run-ins with the NUS at the protest

IMAGE: NUS National President gets down with the students at the 10th November anti-cuts demo

and their official post-protest statements criminalising the direct action by attributing it to a few infiltrating anarchists who ruined a peaceful demonstration exceeded my previous suspicions. The NUS is not a useless, defunct organisation; it is media powerful and divisive. If we begin to attack the NUS, will the big issues be sidelined? Can we continue on with them against us? Has the government successfully divided and conquered? When a union no longer represents its members, and is a corrupt source of power, what do you do? The ultimate question becomes, do you change the union from within or do you scrap it and start afresh?

The NUS has to represent the whole of the student population in the UK, and of course there are various political perspectives on what happened at the protest that need to be taken into account. I spoke to one first year student at Goldsmiths who defended the Goldsmiths Student Union's (GSU) official statement reprimanding Millbank protestors. She said she watched a lot of footage of what happened and felt the protestors were 'mean to the police officers that were defenseless against the crowd.' She said a lot of students at Goldsmiths felt the same way, and the GSU had to address their feelings as well. As many of the Millbank occupiers were Goldsmiths students, including an officer of the SU who was arrested, I felt a decision based on media portrayals of the events was, well... lame. I proposed the job of GSU was not to be reactive to the students' media-led views on direct action but to help educate so that students' opinions would be well informed. Why not a Goldsmiths Town Hall Meeting to decide where to go with the unions and with future protests? Invite occupiers to answer questions and explain their experience and invite the local Liberal Democrat MP, Simon Hughes, to answer questions on the cuts.

Another suggestion is to look at the New York Taxi Alliance. After decades of neglect by defunct and corrupt unions that were out of touch with the workers, a new more radical, more demanding union emerged. The New York Taxi Alliance has successfully built to become the largest taxi union in the city and now collaborates with taxi unions internationally. Through direct action and protest they were able to substantially change their wages and rights for the better. Perhaps we can learn from this.

Students are in a precarious position. We are not asking for worker's rights. If we don't go to school, economic production will not be halted. The

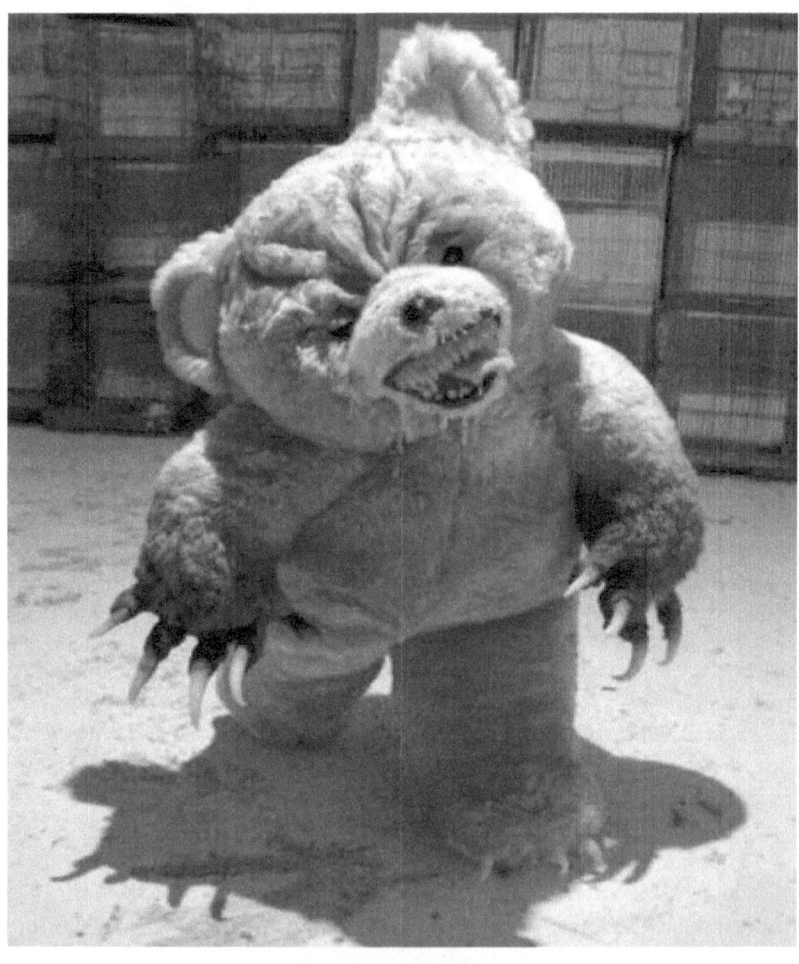

effects of the cuts will be a slower, more gradual change in British society. The university will be turning out a different type of student, one that views her education as not the development of her mind, but as a means to a capitalist end. It will look like the American system. The most common question a student

IMAGE: Under the Clegg, the beast?

studying the humanities will receive is 'What are you going to do with that?' not 'What are you learning about?'

What are the effects of the American system on American society? The American system creates an underlying anti-political sentiment limiting the boundaries most students feel they can push. As an American undergraduate student protesting the Iraq war in 2003, I made banners, signed some petitions and marched in Washington DC. I did not think to occupy my University. It didn't occur to any of the predominately left wing students in my university that this was a boundary that could be crossed. The political spectrum was on par with most universities in the US (there are a few truly left schools): Democrat or Republican.

As a student protestor who occupied the roof explained to me yesterday,

> I pushed a little and realised we were winning, so I thought what happens if we push a little more, so we did, and we broke a window! Then I thought, wow, we broke the window, what happens if we go inside? Then we got inside! So I thought, if we got this far, could we go further? And before I knew it I was on the roof!

It was not until she pushed one boundary that another became possible. Being crippled by debt, stricter immigration policies, precarious labour trends and cuts in social services and benefits will limit the boundaries we can push. After finishing my undergraduate degree in the US one of my friends went to work at Starbucks instead of pursuing writing. Her reason, 'Starbucks has a great health insurance plan, and I have to start paying my loans back in 6 months.'

Heidi Liane Hasbrouck <heidiliane@gmail.com> is a PhD candidate at the Centre for Cultural Studies, Goldsmiths College

INFO
Charlie Brooker, 'All hail the human face of the coalition: Nick Clegg – sad-eyed defender of the new reality', *The Guardian*, 25 October 2010, http://www.guardian.co.uk/ commentisfree/2010/oct/25/charlie-brooker-nick-clegg

WIDENING PARTICIPATION
BY ANATHEMATICIAN

Despite frequent declarations of solidarity, protesting students and academics are failing to join forces with non-academic staff. Except when police brutality momentarily unites them - writes Anathematician

'Students, and workers, unite and fight!', so claims one of the many simplistic, nursery-rhyme-like chants of recent weeks. For university support staff (and indeed academic staff) the reality is, at times, more problematic. Students are often the ones who complain about us, particularly as fees get higher and they see themselves as having bought the right to a degree and a certain standard of service.

Even students who do genuinely build connections with workers can be selective in the workers they choose. Recently academics and students have worked together nationally and locally against cuts to education. While this is a good thing, there is a risk that they are building what has been referred to as 'an unprecedented coalition of students and workers who used to be students', while excluding university support staff (although, yes, most of us used to be students too). Students have been very active in their support for contract staff on low pay, and have campaigned for better pay and conditions for cleaning and catering staff. Hopefully this will translate into support for university staff facing further outsourcing and redundancies. Some of the student occupations have included no redundancies and the implementation of the living wage in their demands.

However, sometimes I get the impression that for students, uniting with the workers means: talking to lecturers / University and College Union (UCU); campaigning on behalf of low-paid migrant workers; and supporting striking FBU / RMT workers. All these are worthwhile endeavours, but the workers who actually work alongside them day by day in their universities should also feature in their plans. Students' Unions in particular can be

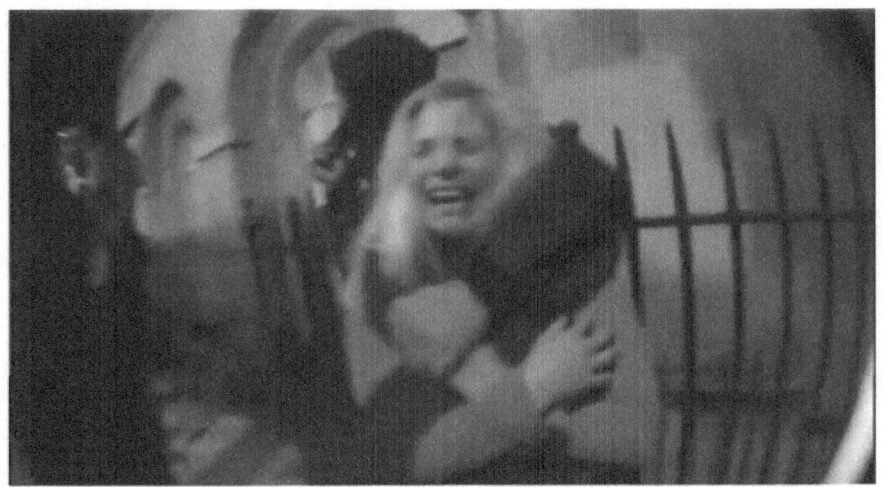

hypocritical, making a mockery of their 'mission statements', and acting as far worse employers than the universities themselves. They even campaign in support of contract staff in the universities while exploiting and / or bullying their own employees. Several London Students' Unions, some of which claim to be 'left-wing', hire HR consultants who advise them on how to sack their workers with impunity, exploiting the fact that the law is stacked in favour of the employer.

Having said this, the problem is not all one sided, support staff can be dismissive of student protests, or see it as nothing to do with them, and the unions have been slow to pick up on and support the recent wave of student protest (to the extent that there is now talk of union branches taking unofficial action, and individuals resigning their union positions so that they can support the students). UNISON issued a statement supporting the November 30th protest ON November 30th! Perhaps it is the lack of interest from support staff and their unions which has led to them being marginalised in the recent debates around the education protests. I have been one of a very small group of people turning up at events and constantly asserting that support staff should be part of this movement.

IMAGE: Pregnant protester weeps from shock after being charged by mounted police, Whitehall, 24 November 2010

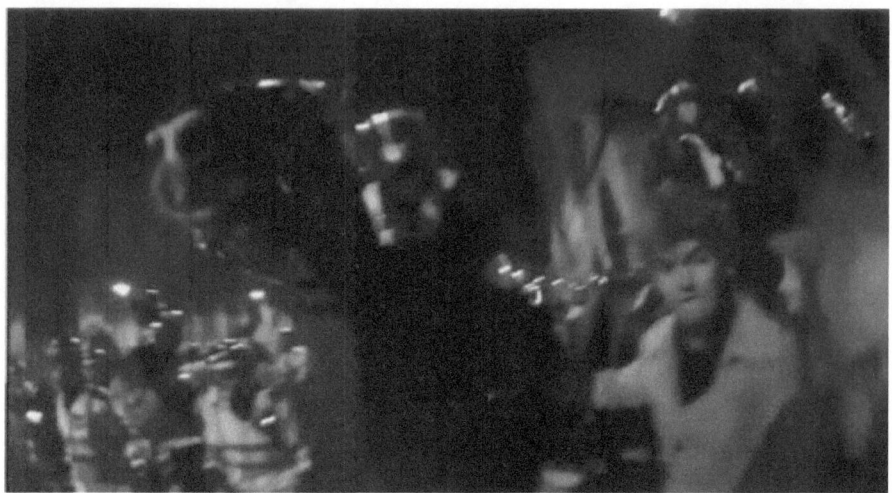

However, there are times when student and worker solidarity does happen, and is a wonderful thing. Wednesday 24 November was a day of action for education, with protests all over the country and all over London. I had to work, but managed to get to two protests during the day. After work I headed down to Whitehall, with a group of university support staff (IT, library and admin) from two different institutions, and the trade union banner from one of our branches. We were going to attend 'a rally with speeches from Jeremy Corbyn MP, Caroline Lucas MP, John McDonnell MP and others'. What we found was something far more interesting - a crowd of young and angry FE and school students, who had been there since the middle of the day, and a lot of riot police, some on horseback. The police maintained that as the rally had been organised in advance and the organiser was here, then of course it could go ahead, and showed us a patch of grass that we were welcome to use, although no one would be able to get to it. Then they proceeded to attempt to forcibly clear both us and the students from the street. No one was particularly inclined to comply with police in this matter. Why should we be? Even in their terms we had fulfilled all the criteria for a legitimate, peaceful protest, and in response they had cut us off from the main body of the protest who

IMAGE: Mounted police charge without warnnig, Wednesday 24 November 2010 were kettled a few hundred yards off, and were now pushing us up towards the Trafalgar Square end of Whitehall.

Over the next hour or so I learned several new skills. The first of these was how to put a trade union banner together very, very quickly, while avoiding teenagers running away from riot police, and dodging police horses and burning placards. This is a good skill to learn, as, once we had it put together, the trade union banner proved very useful. We held it up near the front of the crowd as riot police attempted to force us to move. The students appreciated our presence, they quickly realised how useful our banner was, and used it as something to hide behind, rally behind, or use to hold the line. I did have to dissuade a couple of them from taking the metal bars to use as weapons.

The crowd were very young, some looked 14 or 15, most of them were under 20. There were lots of young black and Asian kids, and I get the feeling that as well as being vocally angry about the removal of EMA, they are already angry at the police due to stop and search. They did wonder what a small group of people several decades older than them were doing in their midst, and some asked us if we were lecturers. We explained that we were university support staff, and why we were on the demo (i.e. sharing their concerns about access to education, but also concerned about our jobs being under threat). They were also interested in the institution referred to on the banner. The universities have failed to recognise the value of this kind of outreach work. If they were really serious about widening participation they would pay us to attend such protests. A lot of these students now want to go to this particular institution. Sadly, few of them will be able to afford it, if the proposed fee increases happen.

At this point something happened which has been the subject of discussion. Let no one have any doubt about this, I was there, in the front of the crowd, and I saw exactly what happened. Police on horseback charged at full speed, without warning, into a tightly packed crowd that consisted mostly of children or very young adults. Police on horseback had been making forays into the crowd for some time. This was intimidating, but we were standing up to them, and refusing to move backwards, other than in an organised way, on our own terms, protecting the students whenever possible. Then things changed. The mounted police backed off and lined up. The police on foot moved off to the side. We thought the mounted police were going to advance slowly, as they had before. This in itself is scary, but what actually happened was something that I, as a reasonably experienced protestor, had never seen before. The line of mounted police advanced at a canter. We had been holding the line all this time, but when this happened there was not even any discussion, we just ran. To our credit, we didn't drop the banner. And we were lucky, there was space to the side for us to run to, where we would be safe from the horses hooves. Not everyone was so lucky. Some of the students would have been trampled if people hadn't helped them, and I have heard unconfirmed reports of protestors being injured. Police are denying that this happened. Police lie.

At this point I managed to make a copper laugh. I had just got out of the way of the horses and was shaking like a leaf, the police on foot were immediately trying to intimidate us further, they shouted 'Can you keep moving please?', I politely replied 'Not really, no!' and pointed out that the metal poles of the banner had come apart and that it was a bit of a health and safety issue, and it would be much more sensible to let me fix them. They actually allowed me a moment to do this.

A funny thing about that horseback charge is that it was completely pointless, everything continued as before, with us moving back but only in a controlled, calm way, making sure that the police did not attack these young people with impunity and without witnesses, and holding our ground whenever it was possible and prudent to do so. Eventually the police backed off a little. At this point we suspected that they were planning to block us off at the other end. We headed down a side street and advised others to do likewise. Those who listened got out, I fear the others got kettled. I hope we meet again, and I am glad we had this episode of constructive, disorganised cooperation, I suspect there will be more to come.

Our next stop was the pub, where I stopped shaking and we laughed about what had happened and viewed it as a lot of fun. It was only much later I realised that we are a bit jaded, and really the reaction to a mounted police charge into a crowd of teenagers should be anger and shock. Some of them were hurt and scared, some of them were brave. None of them will forget that it happened, or that it was lied about later. And I hope they are all back on the streets on 9 December (it has just been announced as the day of the vote on the tuition fee increase) and that we are all out there with them, united, and fighting.

A MUTE MAGAZINE PAMPHLET ON RECENT STRUGGLES IN EDUCATION

INCREASED STUDENT FEES CONSTITUTE A SOCIALLY PROGRESSIVE GRADUATE TAX IN ALL BUT NAME*

*TAKEN FROM 'FREQUENTLY ASSERTED FALLACIES OF THE CRISIS AND HOW TO QUASH THEM'
BY THE MUTE COLLECTIVE AND DANNY HAYWARD

The raising of the fee-cap from £3,290 to £9,000 per year constitutes a risk-free programme of social exclusion, in which the middle- and upper-classes are charged a 'fair' rate for an education that will allow them to reap the economic benefits of employment in a newly desaturated graduate jobs market. The excluded working classes will be generously relieved of the tax burden of supporting their high-born compatriots, while that second group's greater access to education resources will relieve them of the need to compete with or live in the same areas as their one-time beneficiaries. Working class people will not pay for what they will be structurally encouraged not to 'get', unless of course they belong to the category of the meritoriously obedient with the 'desired mind-set'; and the 'diversity' that the Browne Report ceaselessly enjoins will essentially be the reinforced diversity of class positions in a system of ever more differential access to social goods.

Opponents of the centre-left proposal for a graduate tax claim that such a measure faces insuperable 'technical' difficulties. First among these is that it will 'arbitrarily' tax the richest graduates on some of their later income. Due to their reasonable refusal to countenance a £40,000 debt (liable to be auctioned off at some future date to profit-seeking financial institutions), most impoverished teenagers will be unable to become graduates, but this alas does not qualify as a 'technical' difficulty and so remains perfectly tolerable. Meanwhile the Adam Smith Institute tactfully advocates that 'tuition fees' be renamed 'graduate income repayments' as a means of diminishing popular discontent which, with quintessential superciliousness, it believes to be directed merely towards concepts and phrases.

As the UK economy is helped to 'grow its way out of recession', and to flatten in the process all those reliant on state support, the UK HE sector will shrink to fit the plans of a political class who now recognise that 'massified' HE need not be too massified and ought at any rate to resemble a factory more than an agora. Those left in e.g. non-elite English departments will spend their time managing newly prioritised 'student demand' for the Siamese twins of transferable skills training and culture industry pulp, no doubt striving in their 'free time' to demonstrate that their research will issue in new marketable concepts in 'homeland security'. Thus Lord Browne's beautiful image of a 'sustainable' and 'fair' Higher Education system.

For more fallacies and their dismantling, see http://www.metamute.org/en/articles/frequently_asserted_fallacies_of_the_crisis

www.ingramcontent.com/pod-product-compliance
Lightning Source LLC
Chambersburg PA
CBHW030519220526
45464CB00006B/2862